THE MOON

By Emily Kington

CONTENTS

First published in 2026 by Hungry Tomato Ltd
F15, Old Bakery Studios, Blewetts Wharf, Malpas Road,
Truro, Cornwall, TR1 1QH, UK.

A CIP catalog record for this book is available from the British Library.

ISBN 9781835696781

Manufactured in the USA

Discover more at
www.hungrytomato.com

Front cover image is an edited image of an astronaut on the Moon and Earth in the background.Title page image is an edited image of the Moon and Earth.
Contents page image is an edited image of the Moon.

Words in **BOLD** can be found in the glossary.

WHERE IS THE MOON?

There are eight planets in our **solar system**. The planets travel around the Sun. Some of the planets have **satellites** called moons. The Earth has one moon.

The Moon travels around the Earth every 27 **Earth days**. This journey is called its **orbit**.

It orbits Earth from a distance of almost 240,000 miles (384,000 kilometers). That means you could fit 30 other planet Earths between us and the Moon!

MOON FACTS

The Moon is much smaller than Earth, less than half its size. Unlike Earth, it has no **atmosphere**, and no life.

Like Earth, the Moon is also spinning. The time it takes for a moon or planet to spin around once is called a day. One day on the Moon is about 29.5 Earth days long.

The Moon is less than half the size of Earth!

ON THE SURFACE

If you look at the Moon through a telescope, you will see that its surface has mountains, flat **plains**, and lots of **craters**.

The craters on the Moon are created by **asteroids**, **comets**, and **meteoroids** smashing into it at incredible speeds. Without an atmosphere, the Moon has no protection, and these rocks cause explosions that create holes in its surface.

Most asteroids in our solar system come from the **asteroid belt** between Mars and Jupiter.

Some of the Moon's craters have been there for billions of years!

THE FAR SIDE OF THE MOON

The same side of the Moon always faces Earth. This is because the Moon only spins once for every orbit it makes around the Earth!

The Moon doesn't make its own light. It reflects a lot of the Sun's light and this is what makes it seem bright in the sky.

PHASES OF THE MOON

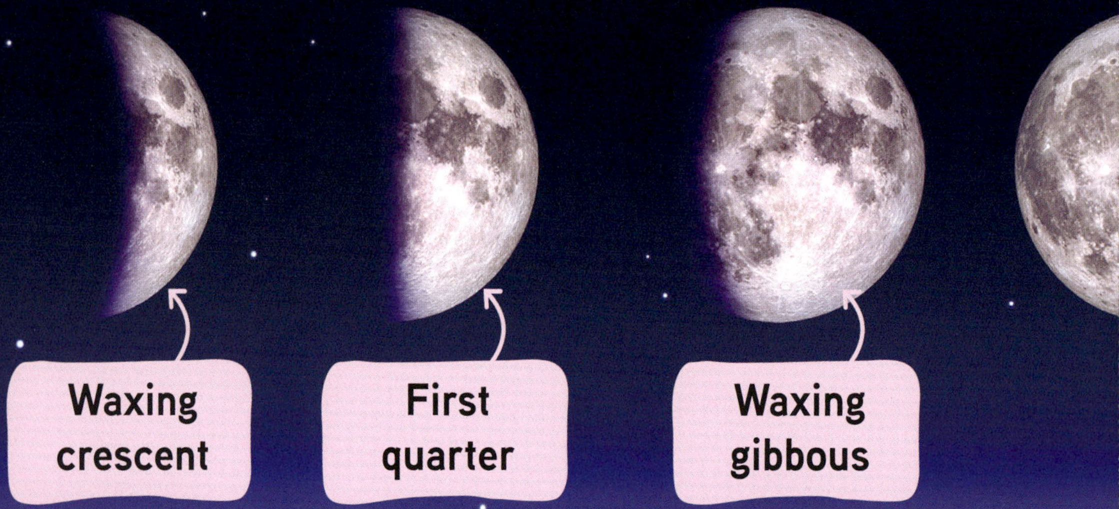

When we look at the Moon from Earth, it can look like it's changing shape. But we can only see the part of the Moon that the Sun is shining on as it orbits Earth.

Sometimes we see all of the Moon, which is called a full Moon. When we can't see the Moon at all, we call it a new Moon.

There are eight main phases of the Moon as it moves around Earth.

THE MOON AND EARTH

The Earth has a powerful force called **gravity** that pulls the Moon towards Earth.

Gravity keeps the Moon orbiting Earth and stops it flying away into space!

The Moon has its own gravity, too. It is strong enough to pull on Earth's oceans and seas, creating high and low **tides**. This means the Moon can move water!

Low tide

High tide

IS THERE WATER ON THE MOON?

The Moon's water is mostly frozen and is lying deep inside dark craters near the Moon's North and South Poles.

It doesn't melt, because sunlight can't reach it. It could be very useful if scientists live and work on the Moon one day.

But where did the water come from? Scientists think that the asteroids and comets that crashed into the Moon billions of years ago left water behind.

TOUCHDOWN ON THE MOON

The only place that humans have ever walked on, apart from Earth, is the Moon!

It first happened in July 1969 during NASA's Apollo 11 mission. Apollo 11's lunar module, called Eagle, landed on the Moon. The **astronauts** it carried, Neil Armstrong and Buzz Aldrin, became the first people to walk on the Moon.

An astronauts footprint in the Moon's soil

The third Apollo 11 astronaut, Michael Collins, stayed in the command module, waiting for Armstrong and Aldrin to return.

Since then, a total of 12 astronauts have walked on the Moon.

Lunar Module on the Moon

MOON LANDERS AND ROVERS

Scientists have created lots of spacecraft to help them learn about the Moon.

Landers are robotic vehicles that are designed to land on the Moon and stay in one place. They carry lots of equipment onboard.

Rovers, on the other hand, are designed to travel around on the Moon's surface. They can be robotic or driven by humans, and are often powered by **solar energy**.

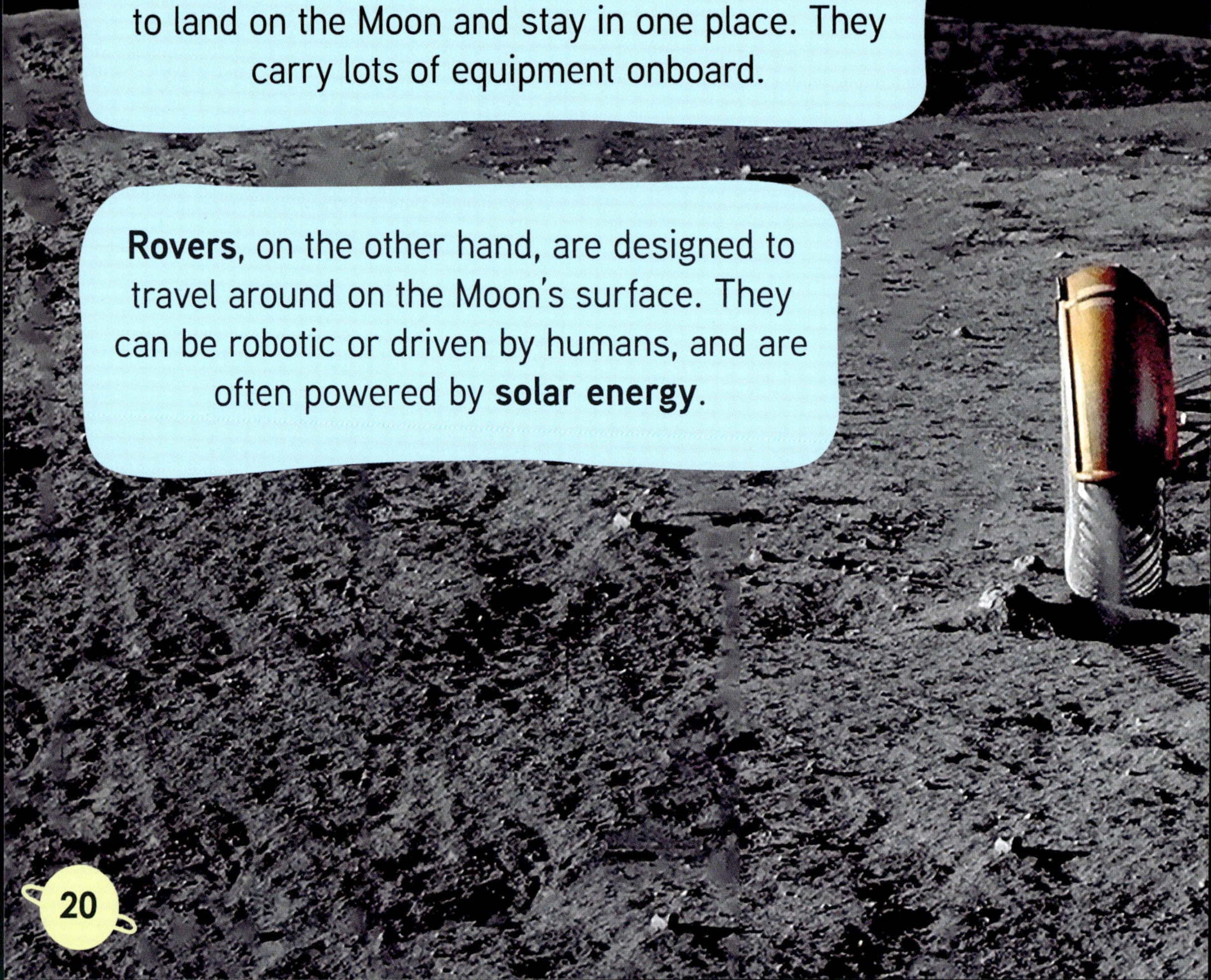

China's Chang'e 6 mission had both a lander and a rover. It was able to collect samples of rock and soil and return them safely to Earth!

Chang'e 6

WHAT'S NEXT?

Will we ever live on the Moon? Since 1972, no humans have been back to the Moon. But there are plans to go soon...

There is hope that we can one day build a **moon base**, so that scientists can stay and work there.

For humans, being in space can affect muscles and bones, and even change the shape of your eyeballs! Scientists have a lot to solve.

There are lots of problems to overcome as there is no air, no atmosphere for protection, and no food or water on tap.

GLOSSARY

Asteroid belt – an area between Mars and Jupiter where lots of space rocks can be found.

Asteroids – small space rocks that orbit the Sun, mostly found in the asteroid belt between Mars and Jupiter.

Atmosphere – the gases that surround a planet.

Astronauts – people trained to travel into outer space.

Comets – objects made of dust and ice that orbit the Sun.

Craters – large holes that have been created by something hitting the ground.

Earth days – the amount of time a day lasts for on Earth (24 hours).

Gravity – an invisible force that pulls things together. Gravity keeps our feet on the ground and the planets spinning around the Sun.

Landers – spacecraft designed to land on the surface of other planets.

Meteoroids – small natural objects, such as rocks or metals, that travel through outer space.

Moon base – a place built on the Moon where people can live, work, and conduct science experiments.

Orbit – the path taken by one object circling around another object in space.

Plains – large, flat areas of land.

Reflects – to shine back.

Rovers – robotic vehicles designed to explore the surfaces of other planets or moons.

Satellites – things that orbit around a planet. They can be natural, like the Moon, or human-made.

Solar energy – energy that comes from the Sun.

Solar system – The Sun and everything that moves around it.

Tides – the rising and falling of sea levels.

Picture credits:
(t=top; b=bottom; m=middle; l=left; r=right):

NASA: images-assets.nasa.gov/image/6901250/6901250~orig.jpg 18bl; images-assets.nasa.gov/image/as14-66-09277/as14-66-09277~orig.jpg 19tr. Wikipedia: By China National Space Administration - China National Space administration social media account, Fair use 21tr. Shutterstock: Artsiom P 18-19bg, 20-21bg; Berni0004 1bg; Corona Borealis Studio 22-23bg; dam_point 14-15bg; Design projects 8-9bg; Dima zel 6bl, 16-17bg; Iva Foto 4-5bg; HelenField 9tr; Juergen Faelchle 6-7bg; MartiBStock 17mr; mattL_Images 12-13bg; Mozzy b 9tl; multishooter 15tr, 15tl; Pike-28 10-11bg; Procy 24bg; Somchai Som 2-3bg.